Forest Friends

INTRODUCTION

I love nature and wildlife, so this book has been a lot of fun creating critters from the woodlands. n a springtime hike in the mountains, along streams, through forests and grasses, you could easily spy any one of these est friends frolicking nearby. Do you have a favorite memory of the first time your child pointed out a little animal? Were ey in awe about the creature's beauty? An array of flowers in my favorite colors helps to give each of these critters their own distinct character. I am so excited to share this book with you! I hope you enjoy making the entire set for yourself, your little one, as a gift, or all the above. Having these little animals around will remind us all of scenes from the trail, even from home.

LEISURE ARTS, INC. • Maumelle, Arkansas

TABLE OF CONTENTS

MEET CHEYANNE VALENCIA

I am a crafter and fiber artist living in Montana and I especially enjoy needle arts. Embroidery is my favorite medium, and I've been doing it since I was a girl. Creative needle art is a relaxing and very fulfilling way to spend my time. I hope to continue to do it for many years to come. In today's fast paced and often chaotic world, I highly recommend to anyone...Slow down, Relax and Embroider!

Check out more of my creations and follow me on Instagram, @PrairiePonyMercantile.

DEDICATION

To my mother, who allowed me to play with her sewing box full of wonderful notions when I was small. She taught me how to thread a needle, make a sewing knot, replace a button, and make a hem. And the rest is history!

ACKNOWLEDGMENTS

My thanks and appreciation to my sister, Debra Valencia, for showing me how to hone my creative skills into a professional presentation to be shared with the world. An honorable mention to my favorite nephew, Westin Walker, for his beautiful illustrations in this book. Many thanks to the entire team at Leisure Arts for their guidance and patience during this process.

A

Bear

Finished Size: 5¾" h x 9" w

SHOPPING LIST

- ☐ 13" h x 16" w piece of front fabric
- ☐ 10" h x 13" w piece of back fabric
- ☐ One skein each of DMC embroidery floss (see Color Key)
- ☐ Supplies listed in **General Instructions**, page 42

Refer to **General Instructions**, page 42 before beginning. **Important Note:** Do not cut out the shape of the animal until Step 5!

Stitch Key

1 Flower Stems
Stem Stitch

2 Leaves
2a Stem Stitch
2b Lazy Daisy Stitch
2c Straight Stitch

3 Flower Buds
3a Outline: Stem Stitch
3b Spikes: Straight Stitch

4 Flowers
4a Satin Stitch
4b Straight Stitch, worked circular
4c Seed Stitch

5 Flower Centers
5a French Knot
5b Straight Stitch

6 Eye & Nose
Outline: Stem Stitch
Fill: Satin Stitch

7 Ear & Face Outline
Stem Stitch

8 Body Fur
Seed Stitch

BEAR EMBROIDERY CHART

Color Key

Color	DMC
●	14
●	310
●	632
●	747
●	818
●	893
●	964
●	3747
●	3807
●	3854
●	3863
◌	3863 seed stitch

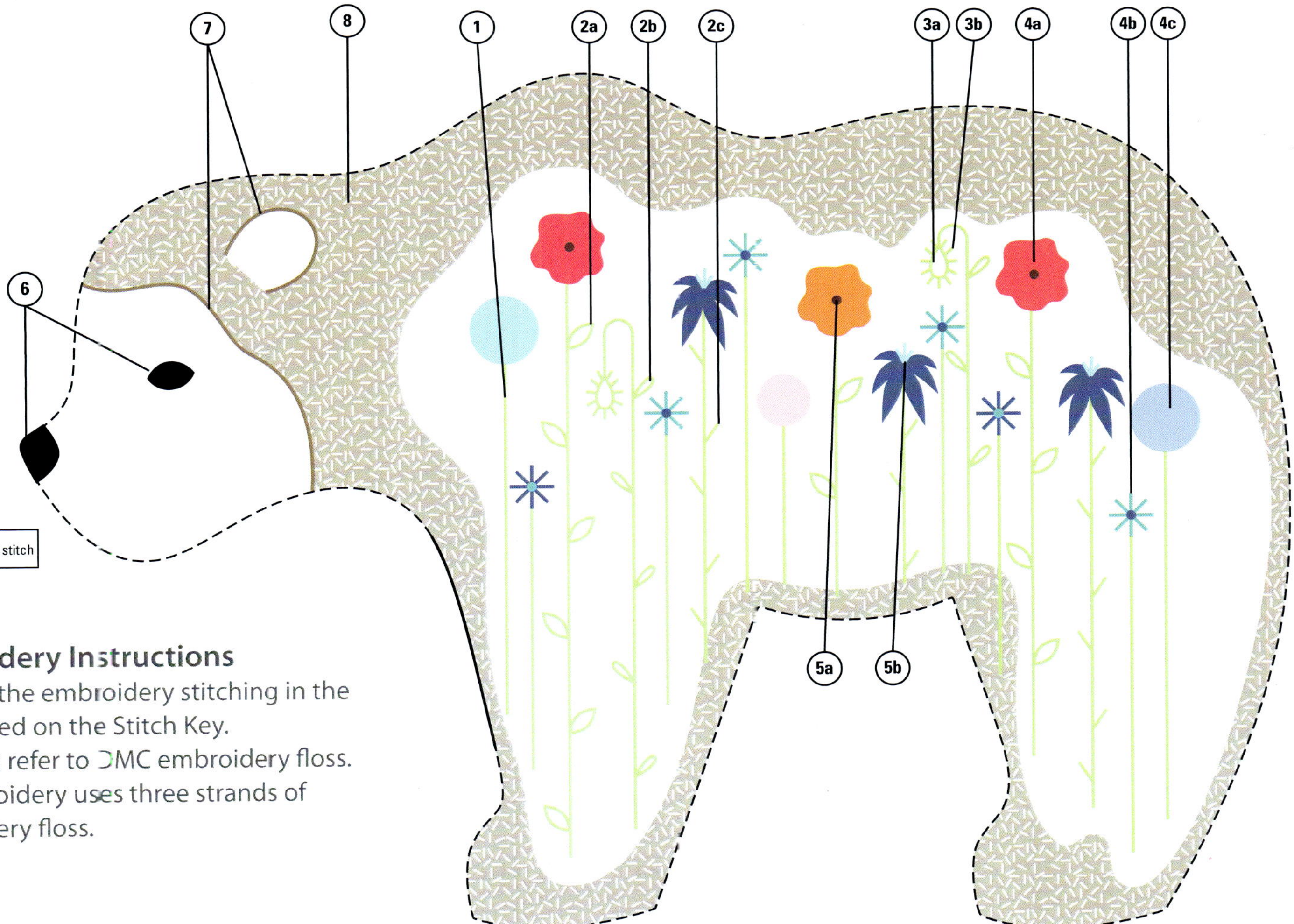

Embroidery Instructions

Do all of the embroidery stitching in the order listed on the Stitch Key.
All colors refer to DMC embroidery floss.
All embroidery uses three strands of embroidery floss.

BEAR PATTERN

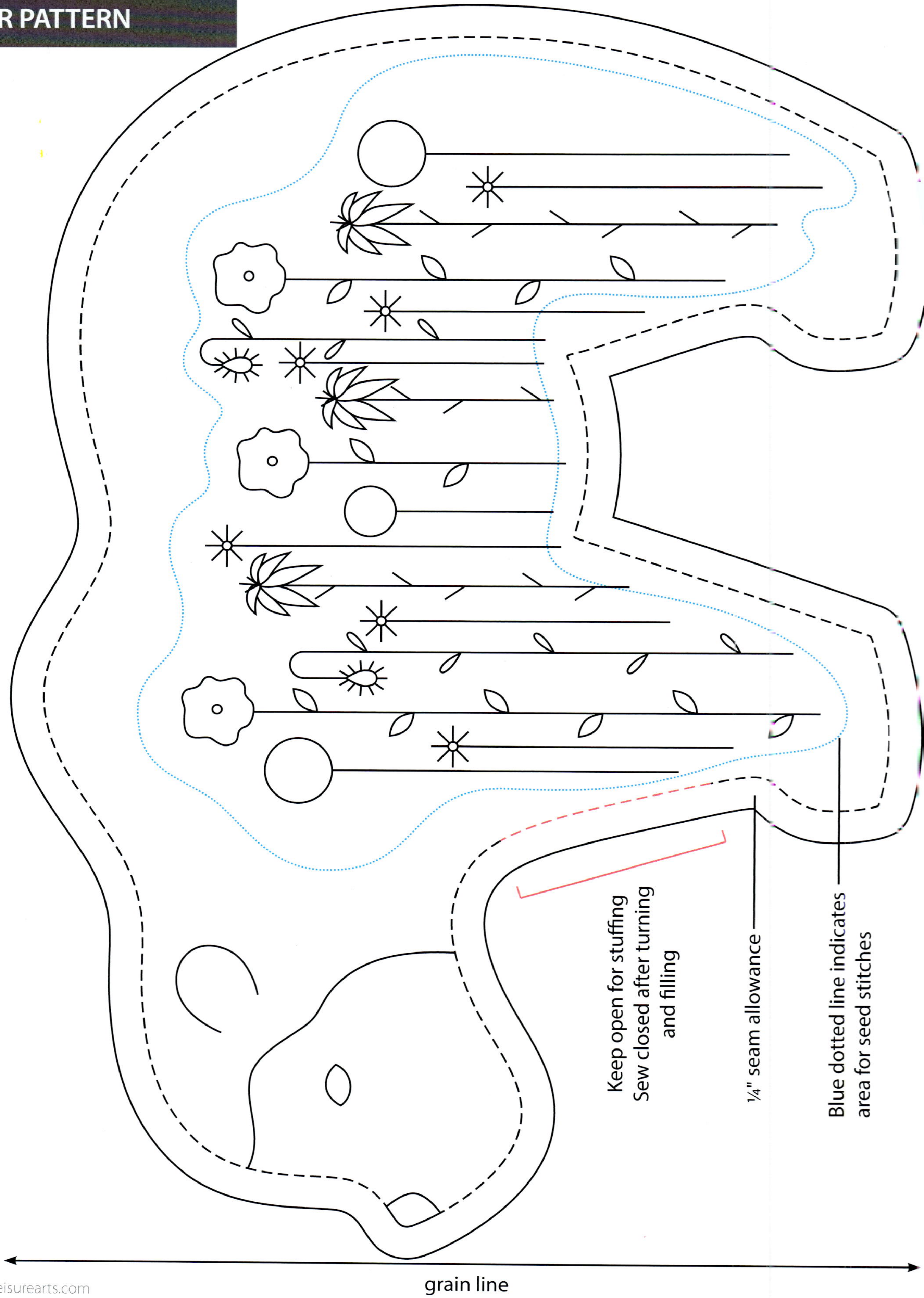

Beaver

Finished Size: 5¼" h x 4¾" w

SHOPPING LIST

- ☐ 12" h x 12" w piece of front fabric
- ☐ 9" h x 9" w piece of back fabric
- ☐ One skein each of DMC embroidery floss (see Color Key)
- ☐ Supplies listed in General Instructions, page 42

Refer to **General Instructions**, page 42, before beginning. **Important Note:** Do not cut out the shape of the animal until Step 5!

Stitch Key

1 Flower Stems
Stem Stitch

2 Flowers
Lazy Daisy Stitch

3 Flower Centers
French Knot

4 Eyes
French Knot

5 Nose
Outline: Stem Stitch
Fill: Satin Stitch

6 Upper Lip
Stem Stitch (Stitch between the teeth later.)

7 Teeth
Outline: Stem Stitch
Fill: Satin Stitch

8 Bumble Bee Body
Satin Stitch

9 Bumble Bee Wings
Lazy Daisy Stitch

10 Bumble Bee Antennae
Straight Stitch

11 Hands Outline
Stem Stitch

12 Tail Texture
Stem Stitch

13 Muzzle & Neck Fur
Seed Stitch

14 Face & Body Fur
Seed Stitch

15 Teeth Split
Straight Stitch

BEAVER EMBROIDERY CHART

Color Key

Color	DMC
●	14
●	310
●	676
●	712
●	818
●	893
●	964
●	3854
●	3863
●	712 seed stitch
●	3863 seed stitch

Embroidery Instructions

Do all of the embroidery stitching in the order listed on the Stitch Key.
All colors refer to DMC embroidery floss.
All embroidery uses three strands of embroidery floss.

BEAVER PATTERN

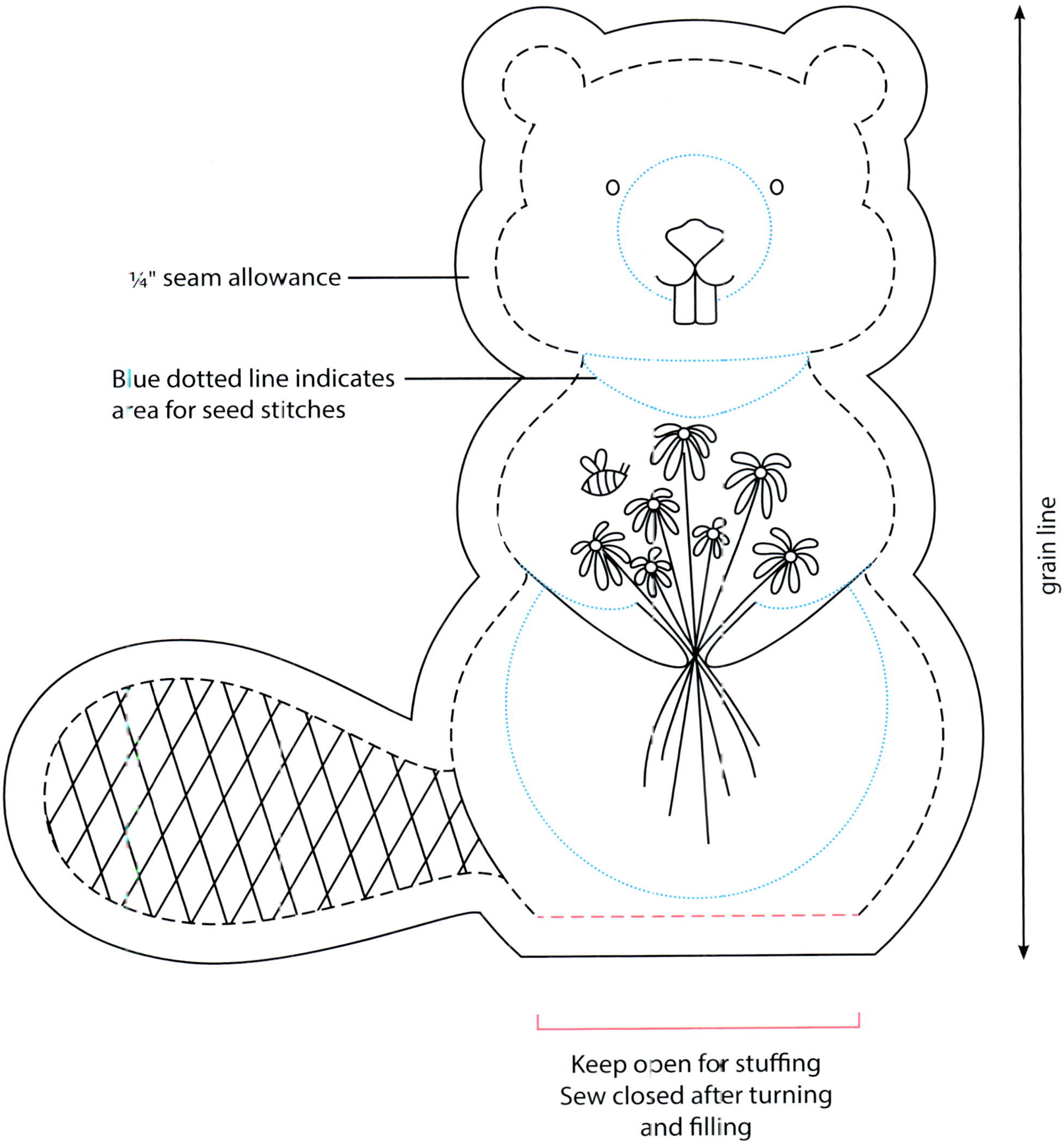

Deer

Finished Size: 6" h x 7" w

SHOPPING LIST

- ☐ 12" h x 13" w piece of front fabric
- ☐ 10" h x 11" w piece of back fabric
- ☐ One skein each of DMC embroidery floss (see Color Key)
- ☐ Supplies listed in General Instructions, page 42

Refer to **General Instructions**, page 42, before beginning. **Important Note:** Do not cut out the shape of the animal until Step 5!

Stitch Key

1 Body Outlines (Hip, Legs, Face and Tail)
Stem Stitch

2 Flower Stems (Including Head Garland)
Stem Stitch

3 Leaves
3a Stem Stitch
3b Straight Stitch

4 Flowers
4a Satin Stitch
4b Straight Stitch, worked circular

5 Flower Centers
5a French Knot
5b Straight Stitch

6 Eyes
Outline: Stem Stitch
Fill: Satin Stitch

7 Nose
Outline: Stem Stitch
Fill: Long & Short Stitch

8 Hooves
Outline: Stem Stitch
Fill: Long & Short Stitch

9 Back Spots
Satin Stitch

10 Ears & Tail
Seed Stitch

11 Full Body Fur
Seed Stitch

DEER EMBROIDERY CHART

Color Key

14
310
632
712
818
893
964
3747
3807
3854
3863
712 seed stitch
3863 seed stitch

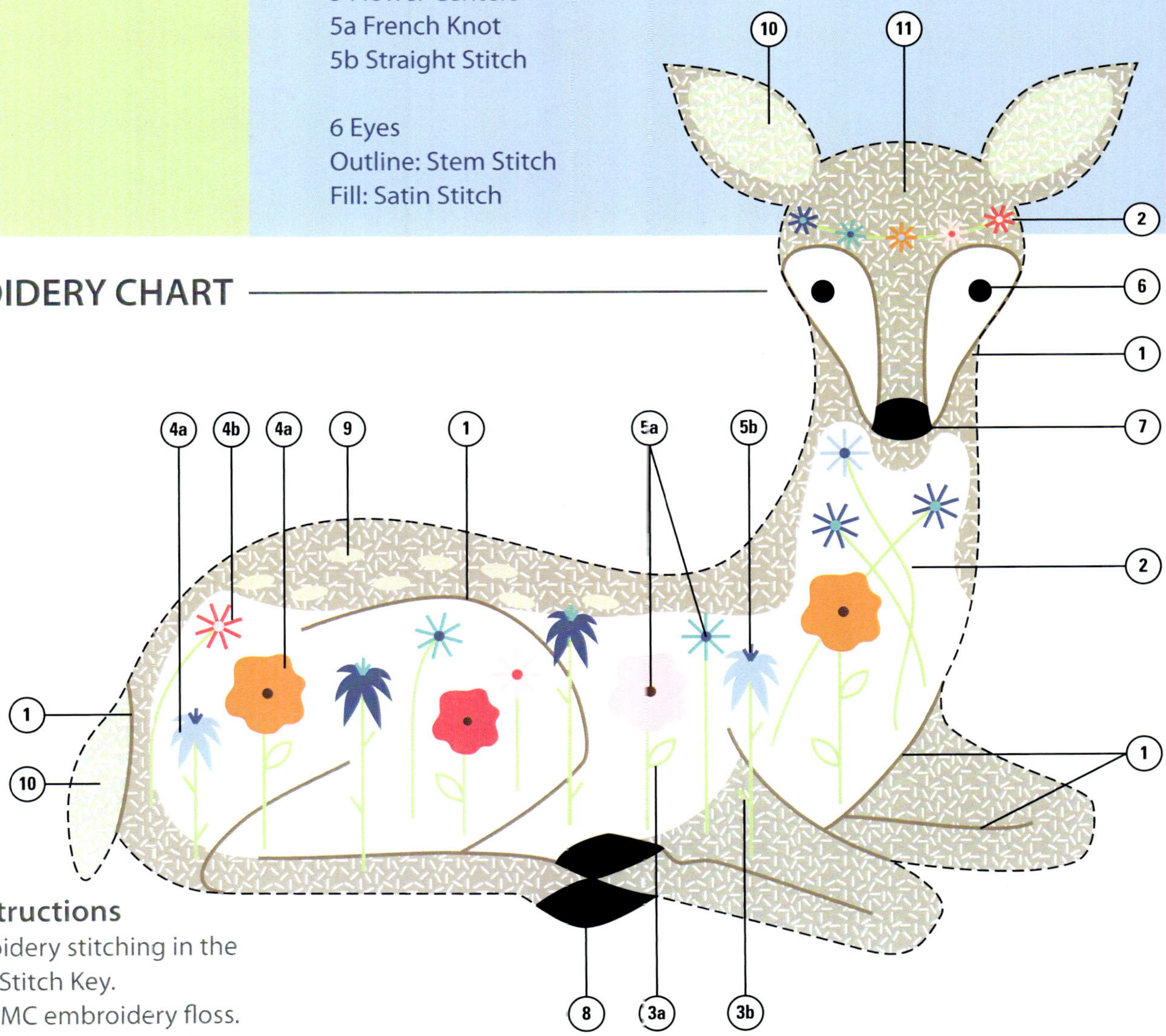

Embroidery Instructions

Do all of the embroidery stitching in the order listed on the Stitch Key.
All colors refer to DMC embroidery floss.
All embroidery uses three strands of embroidery floss.

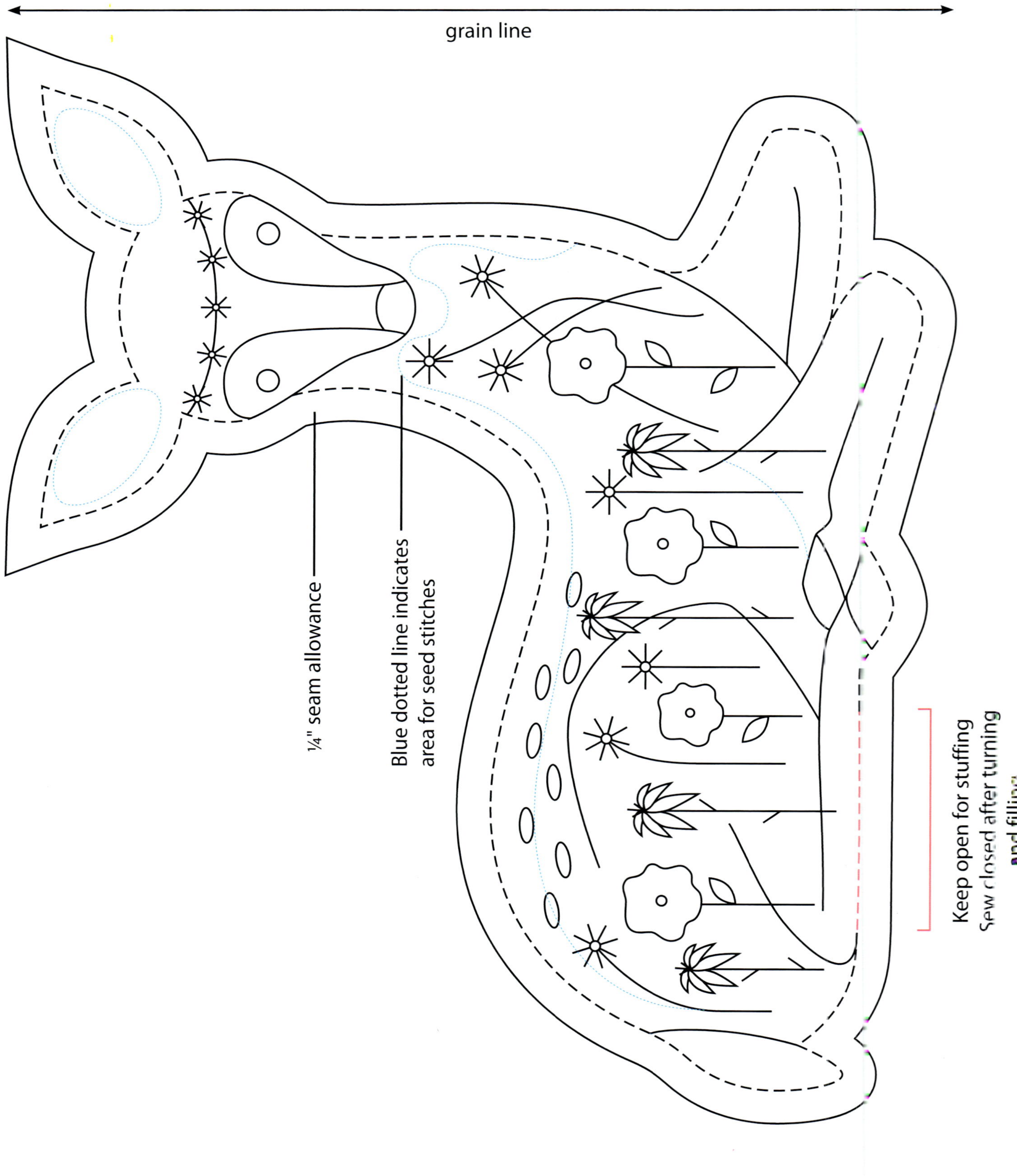
grain line
¼" seam allowance
Blue dotted line indicates
area for seed stitches
Keep open for stuffing
Sew closed after turning

Fox

Finished Size: 7" h x 4" w

SHOPPING LIST

- ☐ 13" h x 10" w piece of front fabric
- ☐ 10" h x 7" w piece of back fabric
- ☐ One skein each of DMC embroidery floss (see Color Key)
- ☐ Supplies listed in General Instructions, page 42

Refer to **General Instructions**, page 42, before beginning. **Important Note:** Do not cut out the shape of the animal until Step 5!

Stitch Key

1 Flower Stems & Leaves
Stem Stitch

2 Stem Tops
2a Lazy Daisy Stitch
2b French Knot, Large

3 Flower Buds
3a Outline: Stem Stitch
3b Spikes: Straight Stitch

4 Flowers
Satin Stitch

5 Flower Centers
French Knot

6 Face & Chin Outlines
Stem Stitch

7 Tail Outline
Stem Stitch

8 Eyes
French Knot

9 Nose
Outline: Stem Stitch
Fill: Satin Stitch

10 Ear Tips & Paws
Seed Stitch

11 Head & Tail Fur
Seed Stitch

FOX EMBROIDERY CHART

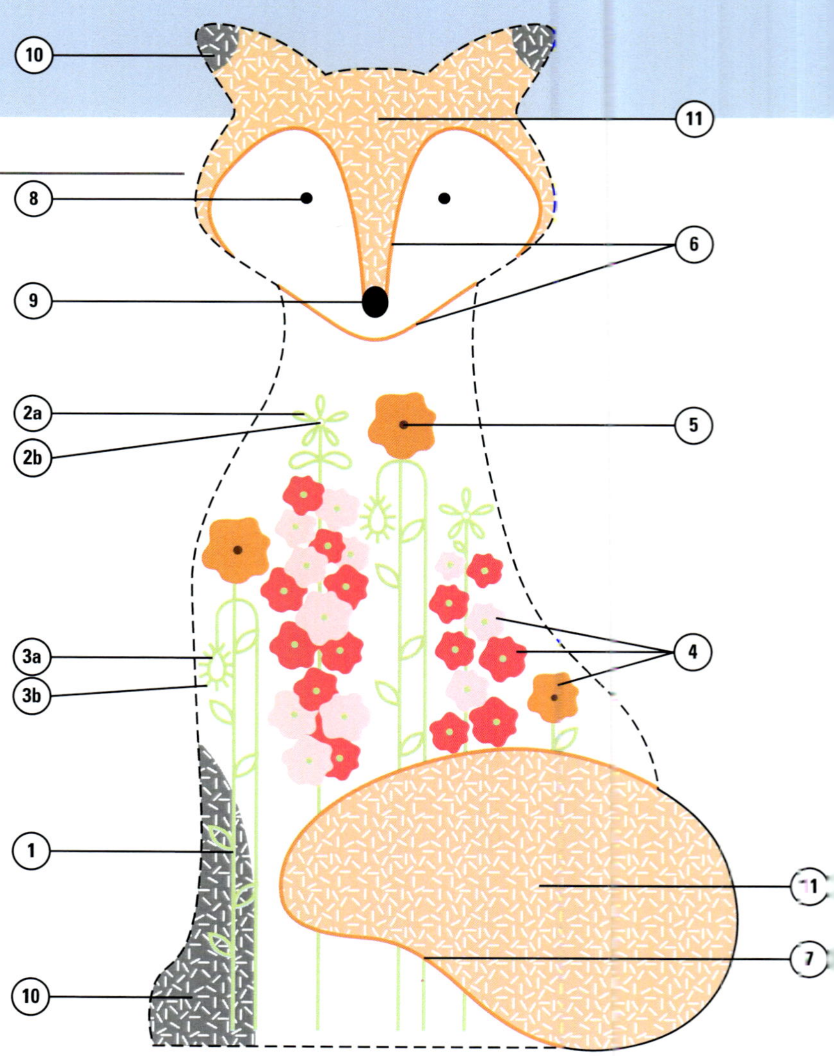

Color Key

(light green)	14
(black)	310
(brown)	632
(pink)	818
(red)	893
(orange)	3854
(gray pattern)	310 seed stitch
(orange pattern)	3854 seed stitch

Embroidery Instructions

Do all of the embroidery stitching in the order listed on the Stitch Key.
All colors refer to DMC embroidery floss.
All embroidery uses three strands of embroidery floss.

FOX PATTERN

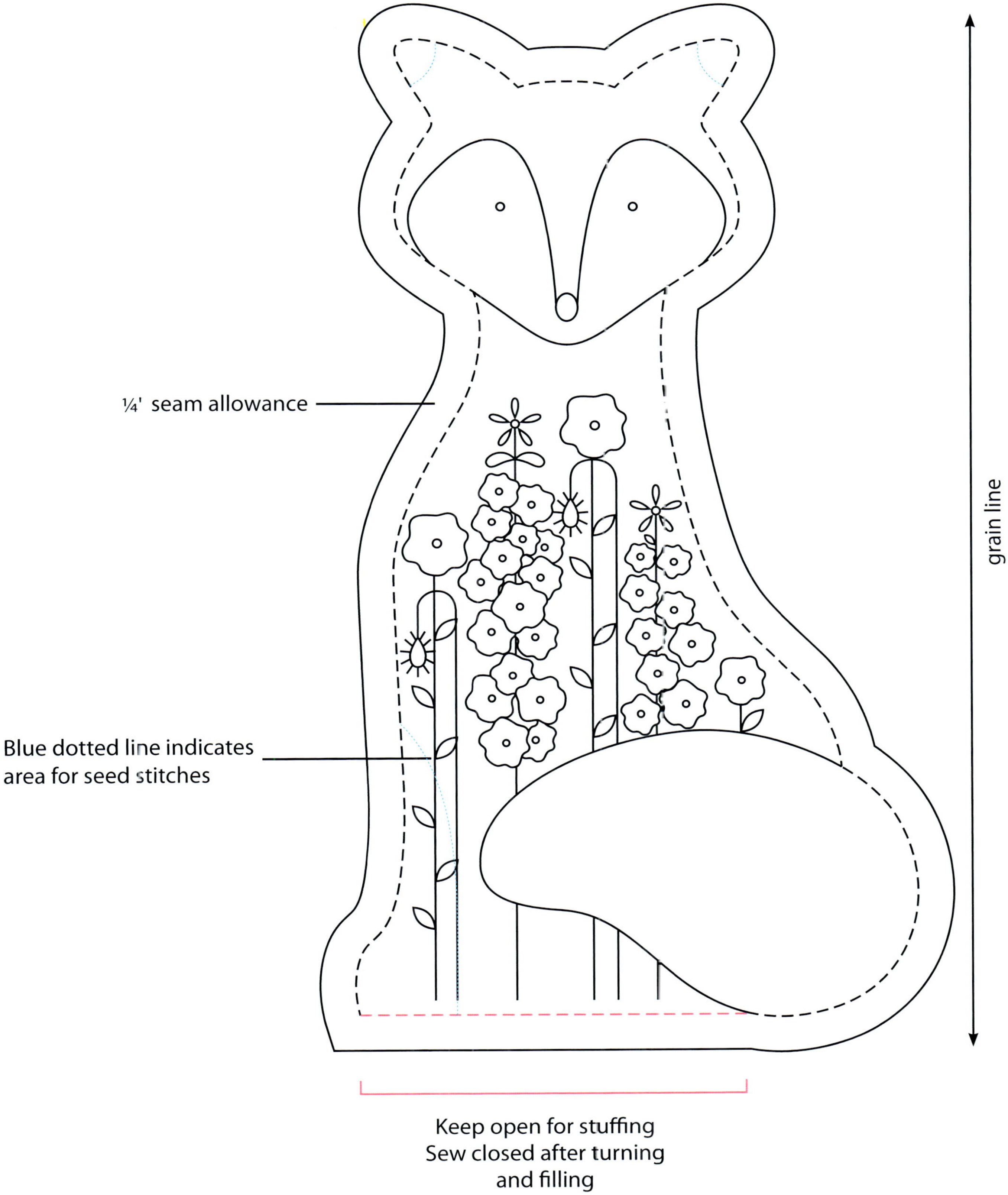
¼' seam allowance
Blue dotted line indicates area for seed stitches
grain line
Keep open for stuffing
Sew closed after turning
and filling

Hummingbird

Finished Size: 3½" h x 3½" w

SHOPPING LIST

- ☐ 10" h x 10" w piece of front fabric
- ☐ 8" h x 8" w piece of back fabric
- ☐ One skein each of DMC embroidery floss (see Color Key)
- ☐ Supplies listed in General Instructions, page 42

Refer to **General Instructions**, page 42, before beginning. **Important Note:** Do not cut out the shape of the animal until Step 5!

Stitch Key

1 Body Outline
Stem Stitch

2 Wings & Tail Outline
Stem Stitch

3 Beak
Outline: Stem Stitch
Fill: Satin Stitch

4 Eye
French Knot, Large

5 Eye Patch
Fill with French Knots

6 Wing Edges
Stem Stitch

7 Throat Patch
Fill with French Knots

8 Tail Feather Tips
Satin Stitch

9 Wing
9a Wing Body
Fill with French Knots
9b Wing Patch
Fill with French Knots

10 Body
Fill with French Knots

11 Wing & Tail Feathers
Satin Stitch

12 Flower Stems
Stem Stitch

13 Stem Tops
13a Lazy Daisy Stitch
13b French Knot, Large

14 Flowers
Satin Stitch

HUMMINGBIRD EMBROIDERY CHART

Color Key

Color	DMC
	14
	310
	747
	893
	964
	3747
	3807
	3854

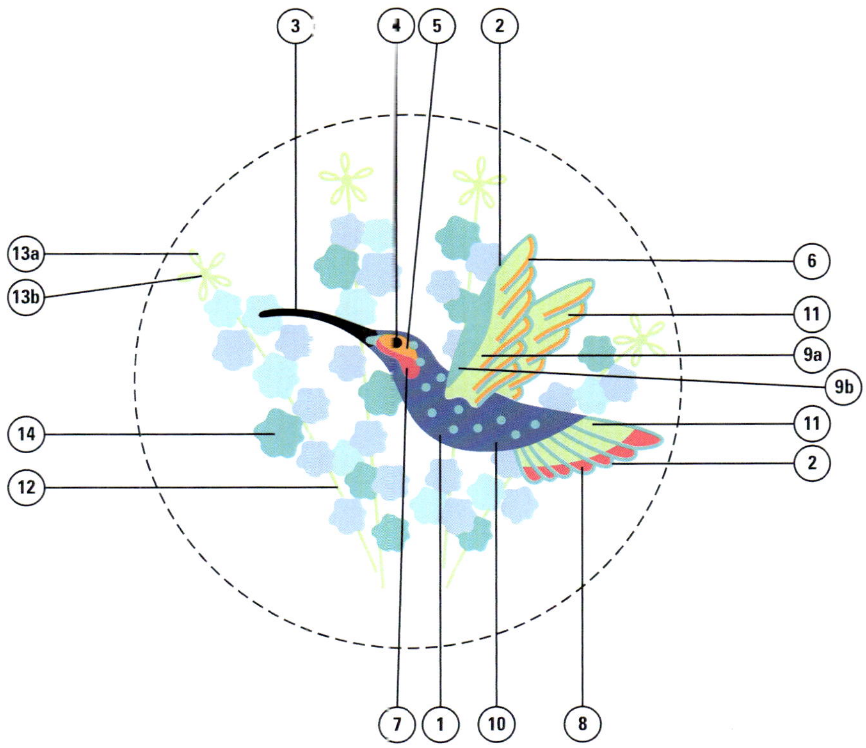

Embroidery Instructions

Do all of the embroidery stitching in the order listed on the Stitch Key.
All colors refer to DMC embroidery floss.
All embroidery uses three strands of embroidery floss.

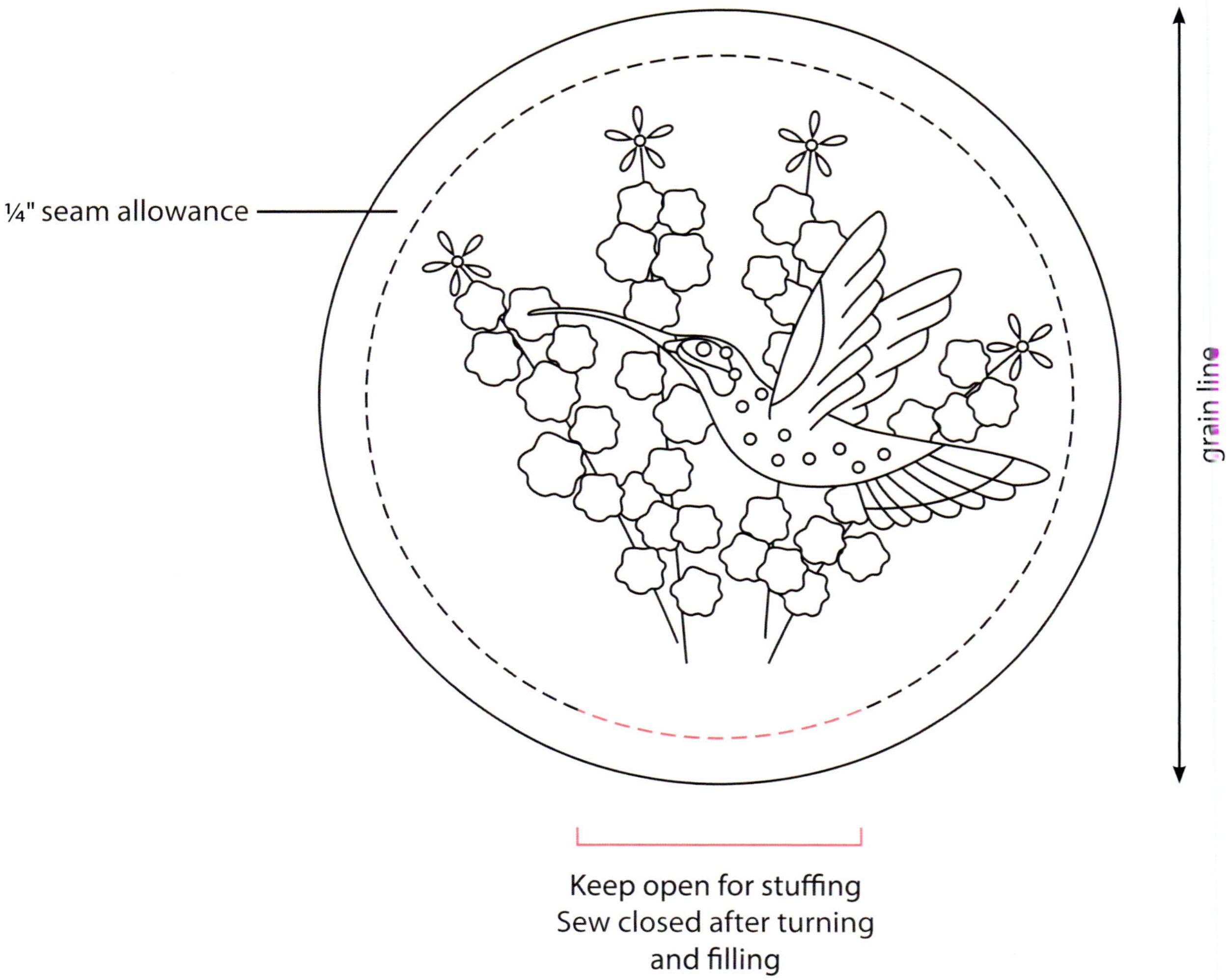
¼" seam allowance
grain line
Keep open for stuffing
Sew closed after turning
and filling

Owl

Finished Size: 5¾" h x 3" w

SHOPPING LIST

- ☐ 12" h x 9" w piece of front fabric
- ☐ 9" h x 7" w piece of back fabric
- ☐ One skein each of DMC embroidery floss (see Color Key)
- ☐ Supplies listed in General Instructions, page 42

Refer to **General Instructions**, page 42, before beginning. **Important Note:** Do not cut out the shape of the animal until Step 5!

Stitch Key

1 Flower Stems
Stem Stitch

2 Leaves
2a Stem Stitch
2b Straight Stitch
2c Lazy Daisy Stitch

3 Flower Buds
3a Outline: Stem Stitch
3b Spikes: Straight Stitch

4 Flowers
4a Seed Stitch
4b Satin Stitch

5 Flower Centers
French Knot

6 Dragonfly Body
Lazy Daisy Stitch

7 Dragonfly Wings
Stem Stitch

8 Dragonfly Head
French Knots

9 Dragonfly Wing Dots
French Knot

10 Beak
Outline: Stem Stitch
Fill: Long & Short Stitch

11 Claws
Stem Stitch

12 Eyes
Satin Stitch

13 Head & Wing Feathers
Rows of Lazy Daisy Stitch

14 Eye Circles
Seed Stitch

OWL EMBROIDERY CHART

Color Key

Color	DMC
●	14
●	632
●	676
●	712
●	747
●	818
●	893
●	964
●	3807
●	3854
●	3863
◌	712 seed stitch

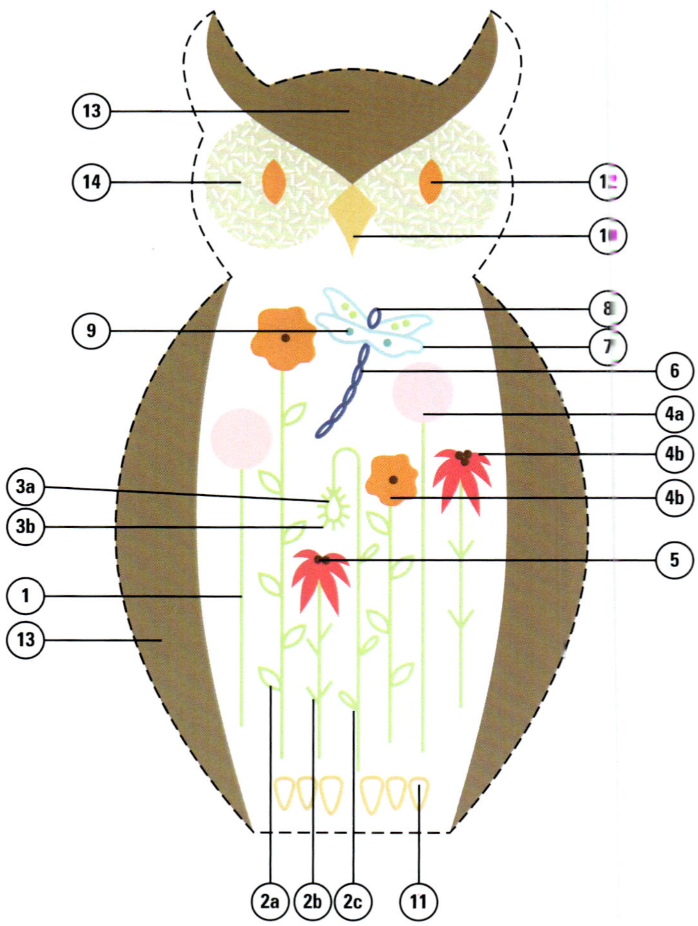

Embroidery Instructions

Do all of the embroidery stitching in the order listed on the Stitch Key.
All colors refer to DMC embroidery floss.
All embroidery uses three strands of embroidery floss.

OWL PATTERN

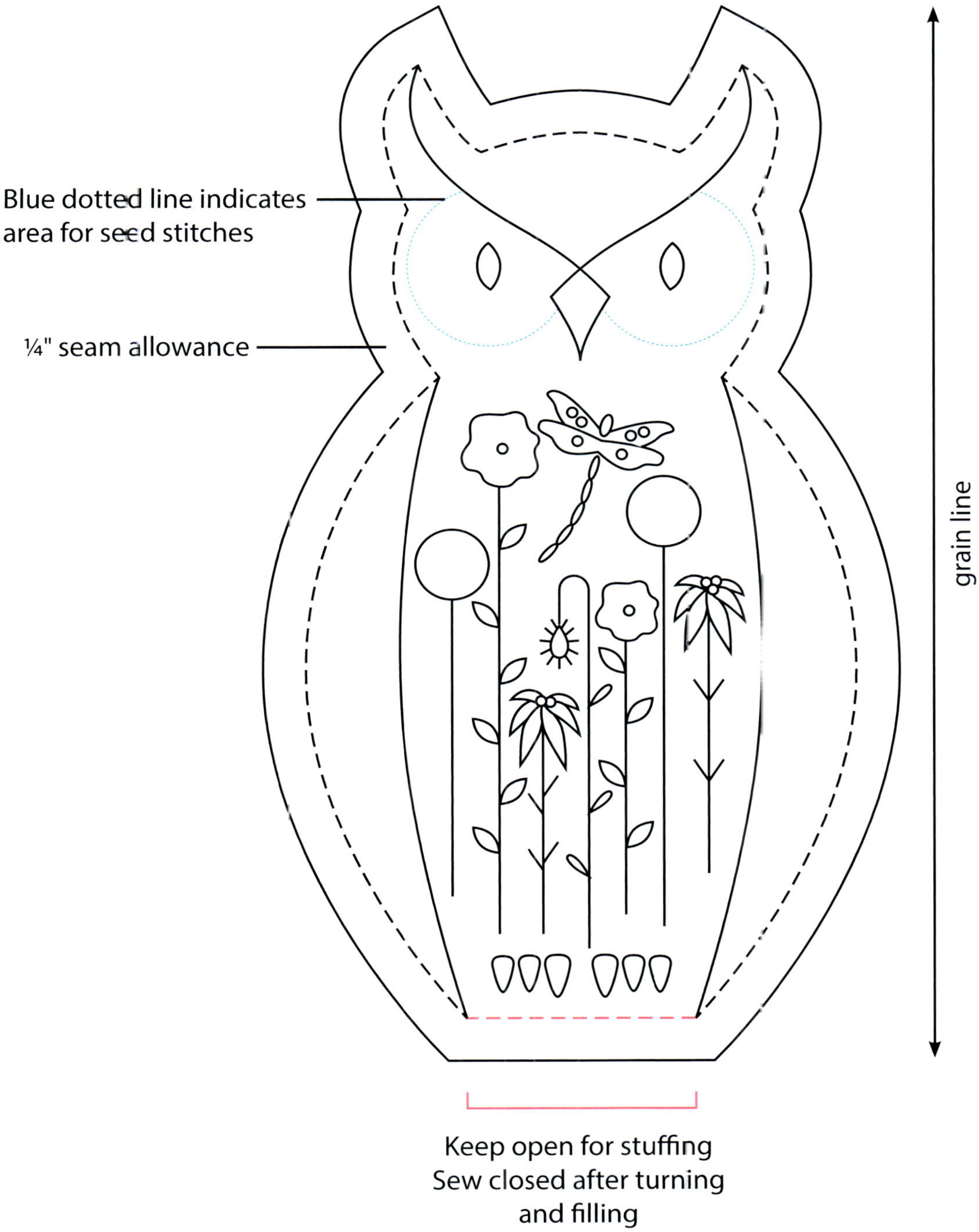
Blue dotted line indicates
area for seed stitches
¼" seam allowance
grain line
Keep open for stuffing
Sew closed after turning
and filling

Porcupine

Finished Size: 3¾" h x 7¼" w

SHOPPING LIST

- ☐ 10" h x 13" w piece of front fabric
- ☐ 8" h x 11" w piece of back fabric
- ☐ One skein each of DMC embroidery floss (see Color Key)
- ☐ Supplies listed in General Instructions, page 42

Refer to **General Instructions**, page 42, before beginning. **Important Note:** Do not cut out the shape of the animal until Step 5!

Stitch Key

1 Flower Stems
Stem Stitch

2 Leaves
2a Lazy Daisy Stitch
2b Straight Stitch
2c Stem Stitch

3 Flower Buds
3a Outline: Stem Stitch
3b Spikes: Straight Stitch

4 Flowers
4a Straight Stitch, worked circular
4b Satin Stitch
4c Seed Stitch

5 Flower Centers
5a Straight Stitch
5b French Knot

6 Eye & Nose
Outline: Stem Stitch
Fill: Satin Stitch

7 Quills
Straight Stitch

8 Ear & Face Outline
Stem Stitch

9 Body Fur
Seed Stitch

PORCUPINE EMBROIDERY CHART

Color Key

14
310
632
712
818
893
964
3747
3807
3854
3863
3863 seed stitch

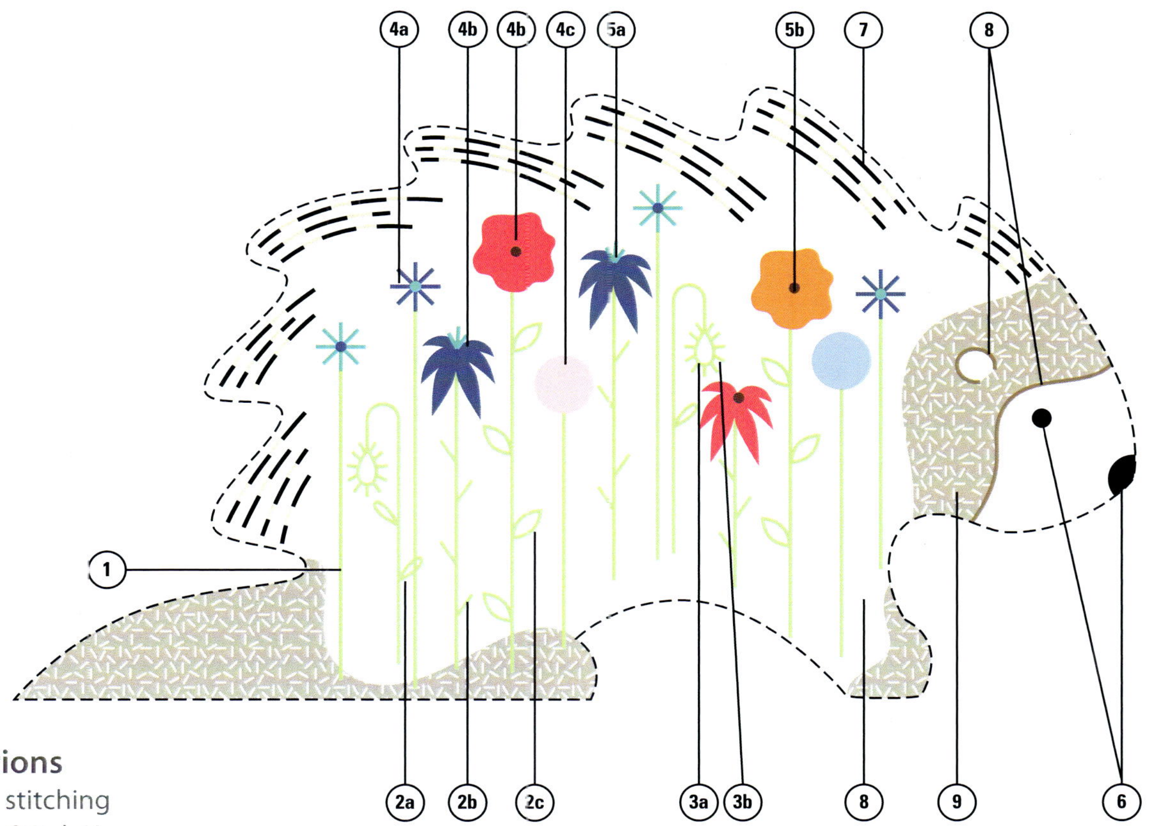

Embroidery Instructions

Do all of the embroidery stitching in the order listed on the Stitch Key.

All colors refer to DMC embroidery floss.

All embroidery uses three strands of embroidery floss.

PORCUPINE PATTERN

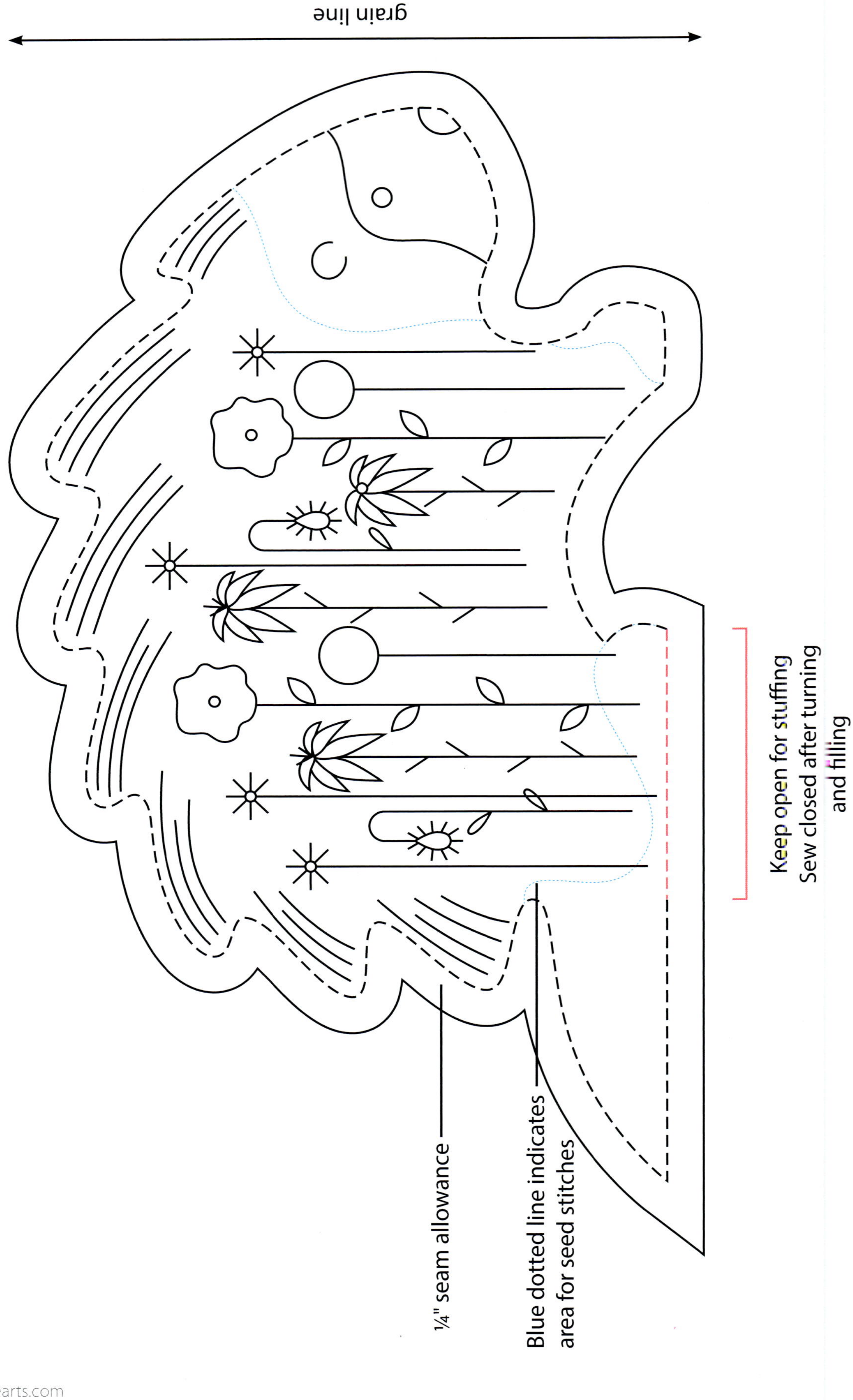

Rabbit

Finished Size: 5" h x 3¾" w

SHOPPING LIST

- ☐ 11" h x 10" w piece of front fabric
- ☐ 9" h x 8" w piece of back fabric
- ☐ One skein each of DMC embroidery floss (see Color Key)
- ☐ Supplies listed in General Instructions, page 42

Refer to **General Instructions**, page 42, before beginning. **Important Note:** Do not cut out the shape of the animal until Step 5!

Stitch Key

1 Flower Stems
Stem Stitch

2 Leaves
2a Straight Stitch
2b Stem Stitch

3 Flowers
3a Satin Stitch
3b Seed Stitch
3c Straight Stitch, worked circular

4 Flower Centers
4a Straight Stitch
4b French Knot

5 Nose
Outline: Stem Stitch
Fill: Satin Stitch

6 Mouth
Stem Stitch

7 Eyes
French Knot

8 Body Fur
Seed Stitch

RABBIT EMBROIDERY CHART

Color Key

Color	DMC
◯	14
●	310
●	632
◯	712
◯	747
◯	818
●	893
●	964
◯	3747
●	3807
●	3854
◯	712 seed stitch

Embroidery Instructions

Do all of the embroidery stitching in the order listed on the Stitch Key. All colors refer to DMC embroidery floss. All embroidery uses three strands of embroidery floss.

RABBIT PATTERN

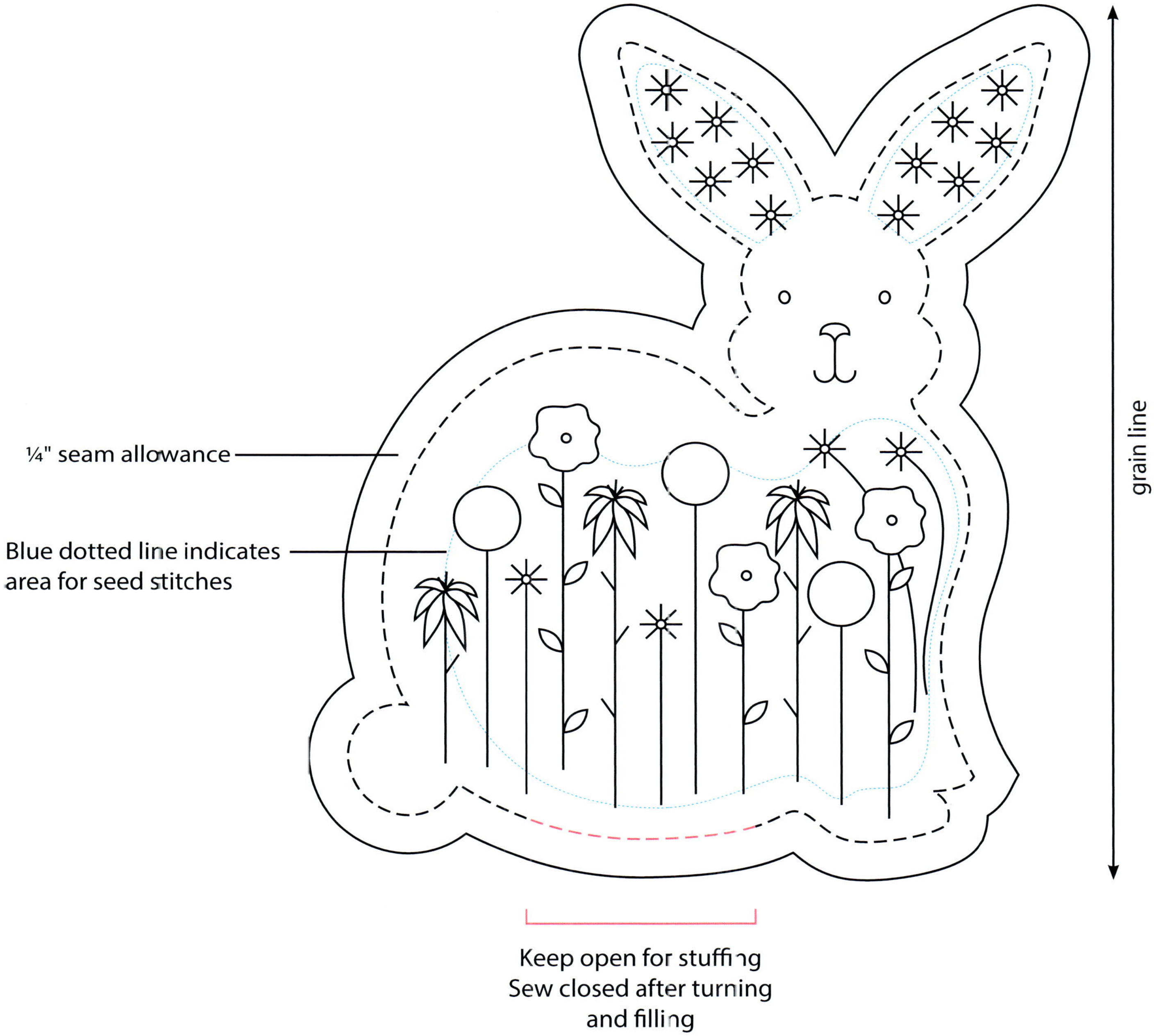

Raccoon

Finished Size: **5¾" h x 3¾" w**

SHOPPING LIST

- ☐ 12" h x 10" w piece of front fabric
- ☐ 9" h x 8" w piece of back fabric
- ☐ One skein each of DMC embroidery floss (see Color Key)
- ☐ Supplies listed in General Instructions, page 42

Refer to **General Instructions**, page 42, before beginning. **Important Note:** Do not cut out the shape of the animal until Step 5!

Stitch Key

1 Flower Stems
Stem Stitch

2 Flowers
Satin Stitch

3 Flower Centers
Straight Stitch

4 Eyes & nose
Outline: Stem Stitch
Fill: Satin Stitch

5 Eye Rings
Stem Stitch

6 Tail Rings
Outline: Stem Stitch
Fill: Satin Stitch

7 Chin outline
Stem Stitch

8 Arms & Hands Outline
Stem Stitch (Can be stitched slightly overlapping the stems.)

9 Eyebrows
Satin Stitch (Arcing over each eye ring)

10 Muzzle & Neck
Seed Stitch

11 Body Fur
Seed Stitch

RACCOON EMBROIDERY CHART

Color Key

Color	DMC
◯	14
●	310
◯	712
◯	964
◯	3747
●	3807
●	3863
◯	712 seed stitch
◯	3863 seed stitch

Embroidery Instructions

Do all of the embroidery stitching in the order listed on the Stitch Key.
All colors refer to DMC embroidery floss.
All embroidery uses three strands of embroidery floss.

RACCOON PATTERN

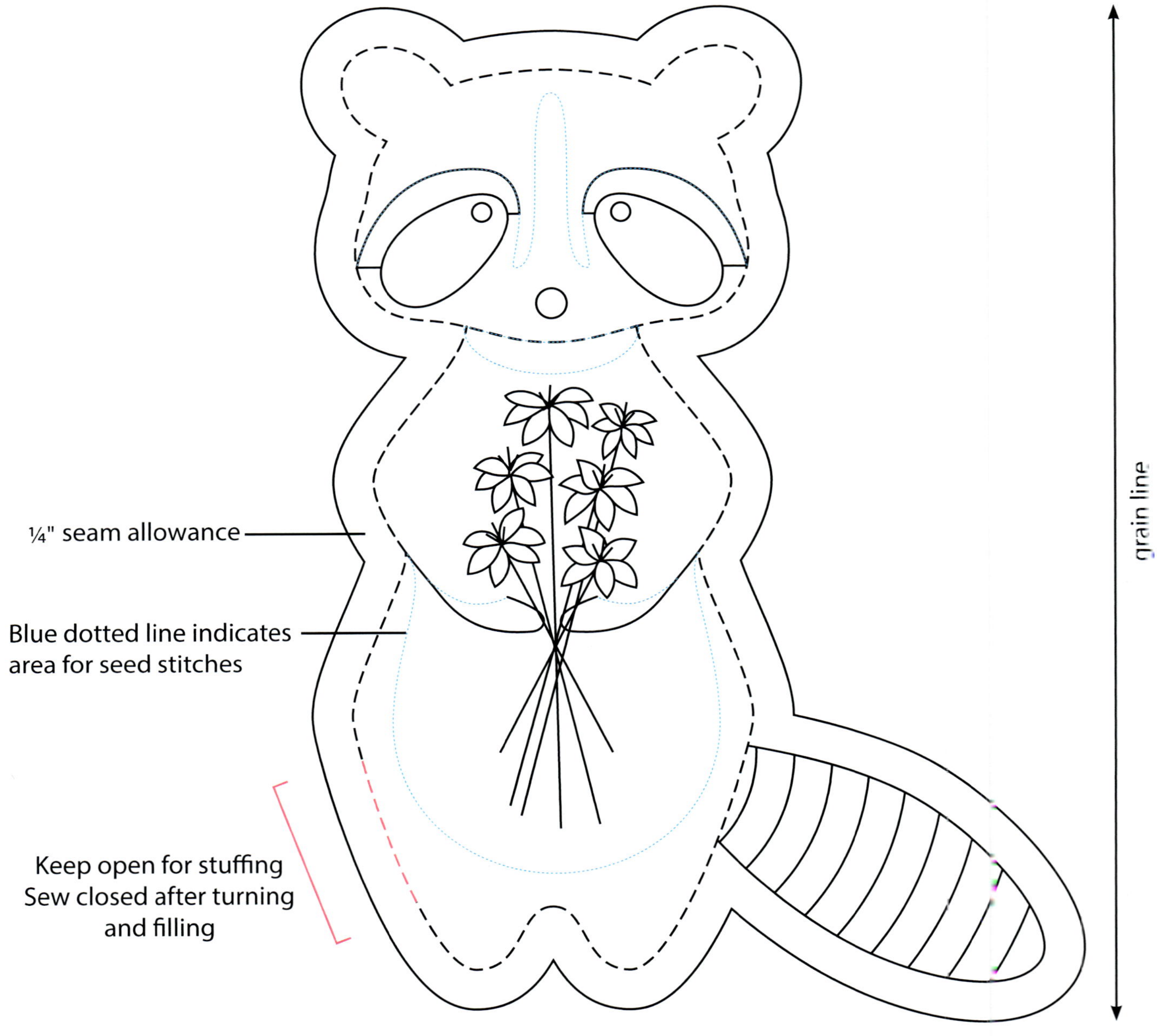

Skunk

Finished Size: 3½" h x 7½" w

SHOPPING LIST

- ☐ 10" h x 14" w piece of front fabric
- ☐ 7" h x 14" w piece of back fabric
- ☐ One skein each of DMC embroidery floss (see Color Key)
- ☐ Supplies listed in General Instructions, page 42

Refer to **General Instructions**, page 42, before beginning. **Important Note:** Do not cut out the shape of the animal until Step 5!

Stitch Key

1 Flower Stems
Stem Stitch

2 Leaves
2a Straight Stitch
2b Stem Stitch
2c Lazy Daisy Stitch

3 Flower Buds
3a Outline: Stem Stitch
3b Spikes: Straight Stitch

4 Flowers
4a Satin Stitch
4b Seed Stitch
4c Straight Stitch, worked circular

5 Flower Centers
5a French Knot
5b Straight Stitch

6 Eye & Nose
Outline: Stem Stitch
Fill: Satin Stitch

7 Ear & Body Outlines
Stem Stitch

8 Body Fur
Seed Stitch

9 Top Stripe
Seed Stitch

SKUNK EMBROIDERY CHART

Color Key

Color Key
14
310
632
712
747
893
964
3747
3807
3854
310 seed stitch
712 seed stitch

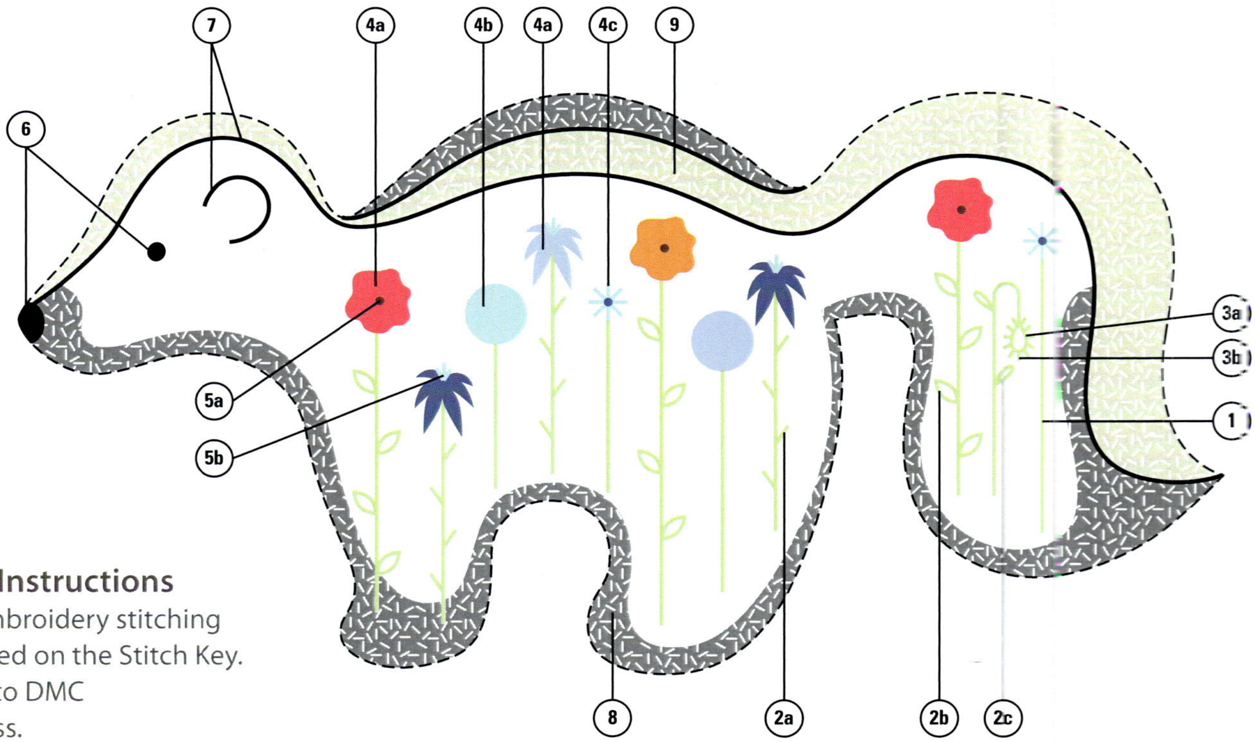

Embroidery Instructions

Do all of the embroidery stitching in the order listed on the Stitch Key. All colors refer to DMC embroidery floss.
All embroidery uses three strands of embroidery floss.

SKUNK PATTERN

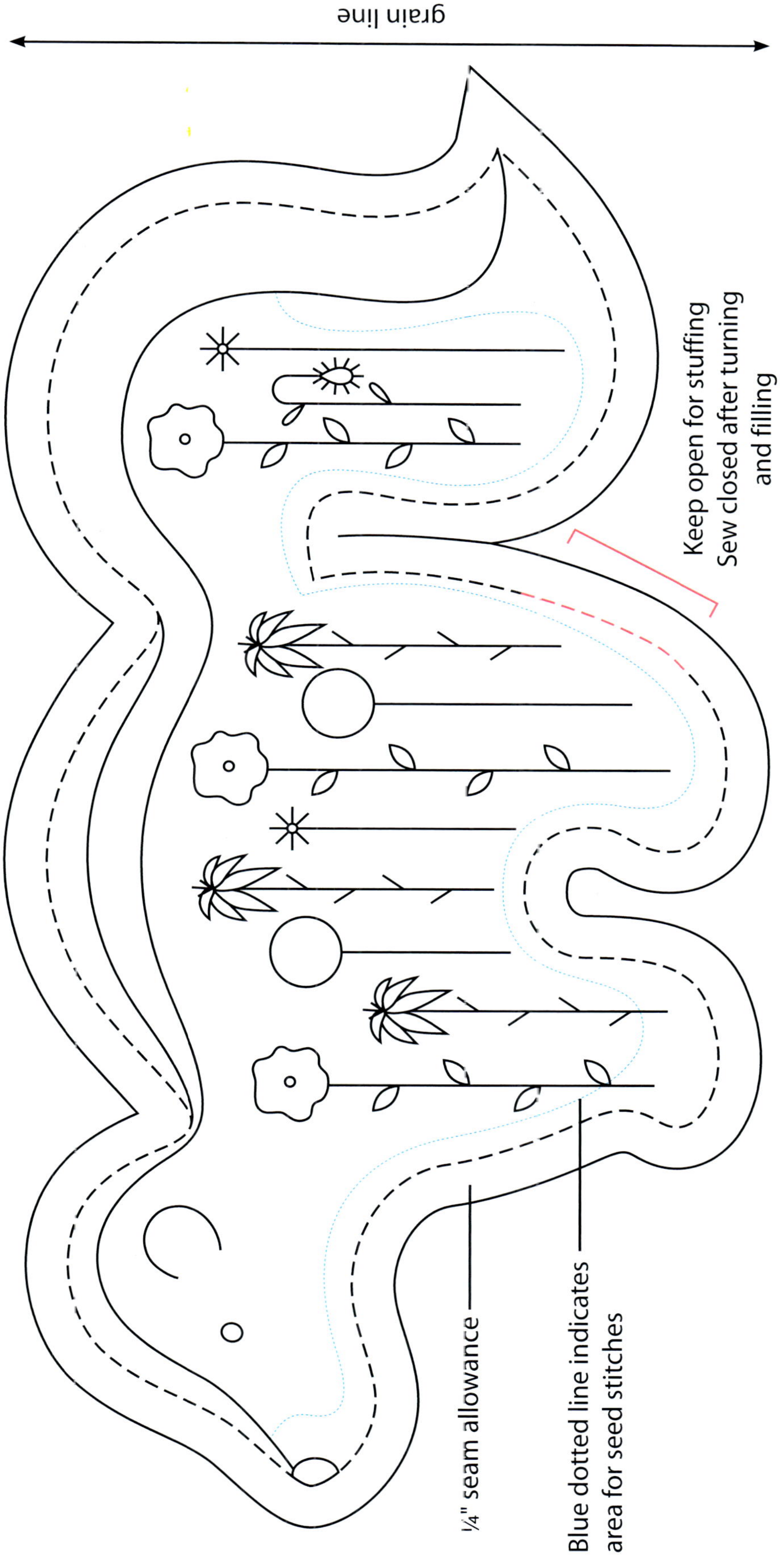

Squirrel

Finished Size: 3" h x 5¼" w

SHOPPING LIST

- ☐ 10" h x 12" w piece of front fabric
- ☐ 7" h x 9" w piece of back fabric
- ☐ One skein each of DMC embroidery floss
- ☐ Supplies listed in General Instructions, page 42

Refer to **General Instructions**, page 42, before beginning. **Note:** Do not cut out the shape of the animal until Step 5!

Stitch Key

1 Body Lines (Hip, Foot and Backside)
Stem Stitch

2 Flower Stems
Stem Stitch

3 Leaves
3a Stem Stitch
3b Straight Stitch

4 Flowers
4a Satin Stitch
4b Straight Stitch, worked circular
4c Seed Stitch

5 Flower Centers
French Knot

6 Eye
Outline: Stem Stitch
Fill: Satin Stitch

7 Nose
Outline: Stem Stitch
Fill: Satin Stitch

8 Eye Ring, Chin & Chest
Seed Stitch

9 Body Fur
Seed Stitch

10 Tail Fur
Seed Stitch

SQUIRREL EMBROIDERY CHART

Color Key

Color Key
14
310
632
712
818
893
964
3747
3807
3854
3863
712 seed stitch
3863 seed stitch
310/712/3863 mixed seed stitch

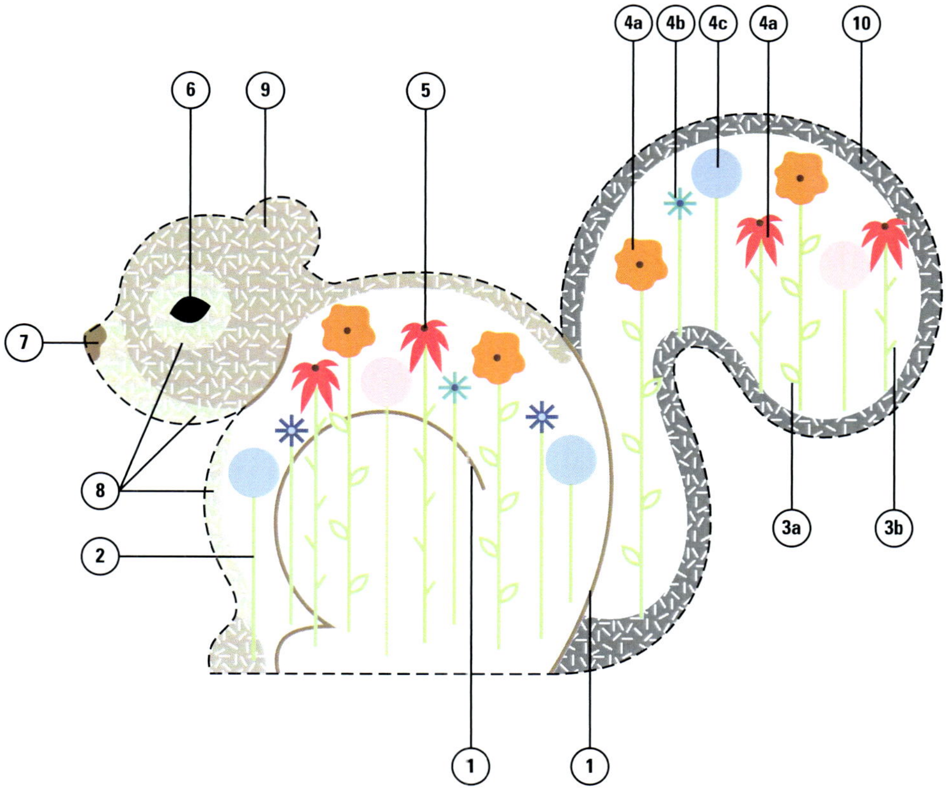

Embroidery Instructions

Do all of the embroidery stitching in the order listed on the Stitch Key.

All colors refer to DMC embroidery floss.

All embroidery uses three strands of embroidery floss.

SQUIRREL PATTERN

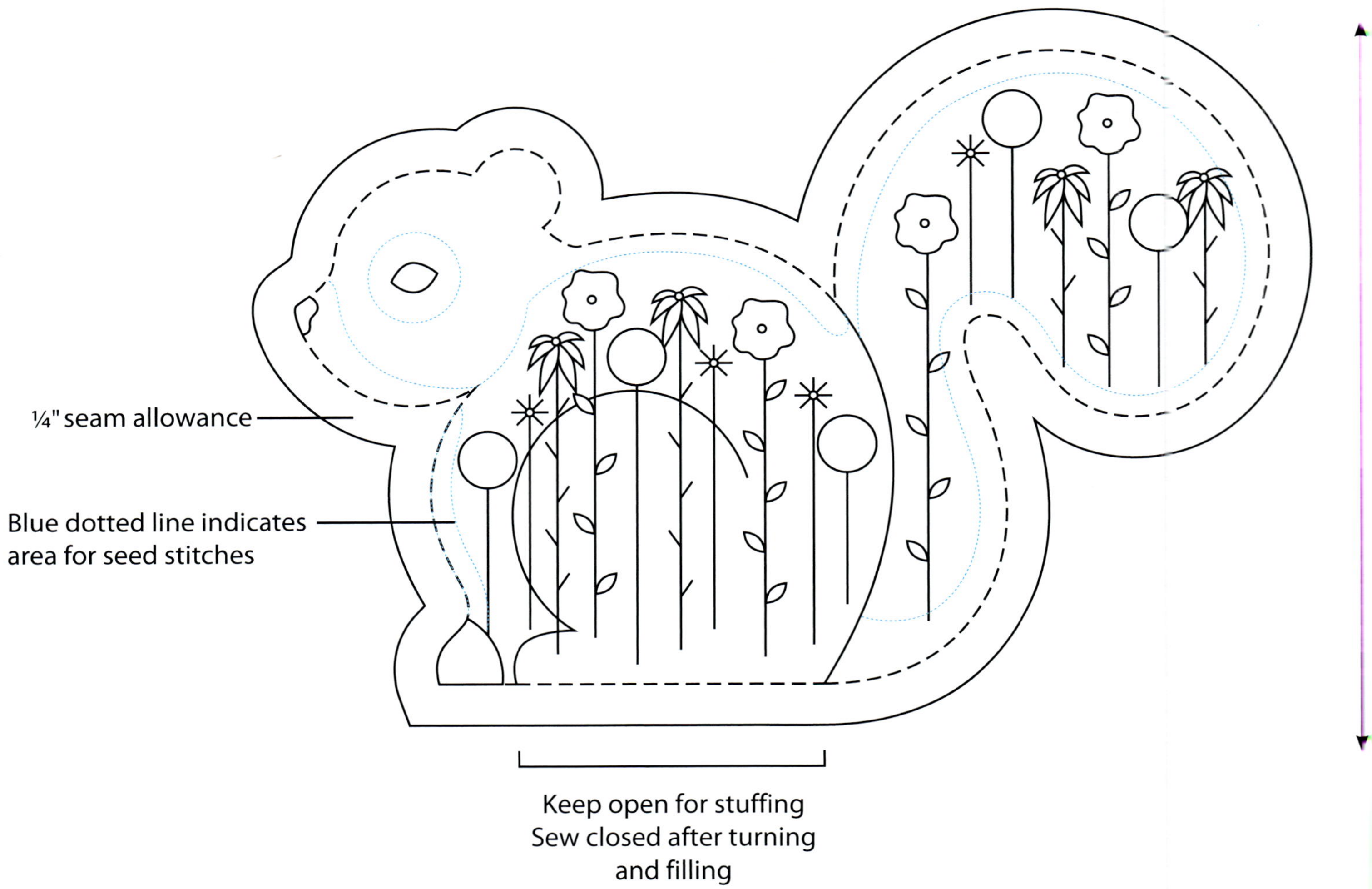

Wolf

Finished Size: 8" h x 4½" w

SHOPPING LIST

- ☐ 15" h x 11" w piece of front fabric
- ☐ 12" h x 8" w piece of back fabric
- ☐ One skein each of DMC embroidery floss
- ☐ Supplies listed in General Instructions, page 42

Refer to **General Instructions**, page 42, before beginning. **Important Note:** Do not cut out the shape of the animal until Step 5!

Stitch Key

1 Flower Stems
Stem Stitch

2 Leaves
2a Stem Stitch
2b Lazy Daisy Stitch

3 Flower Buds
3a Outline: Stem Stitch
3b Spikes: Straight Stitch

4 Flowers
Satin Stitch

5 Flower Centers
French Knot

6 Eye & Nose
Outline: Stem Stitch
Fill: Satin Stitch

7 Ear & Tail Outlines
Stem Stitch

8 Body Fur
Seed Stitch

WOLF EMBROIDERY CHART

Color Key

light green	14
black	310
dark brown	632
cream	712
light pink	818
red	893
orange	3854
gray	310/712 mixed seed stitch

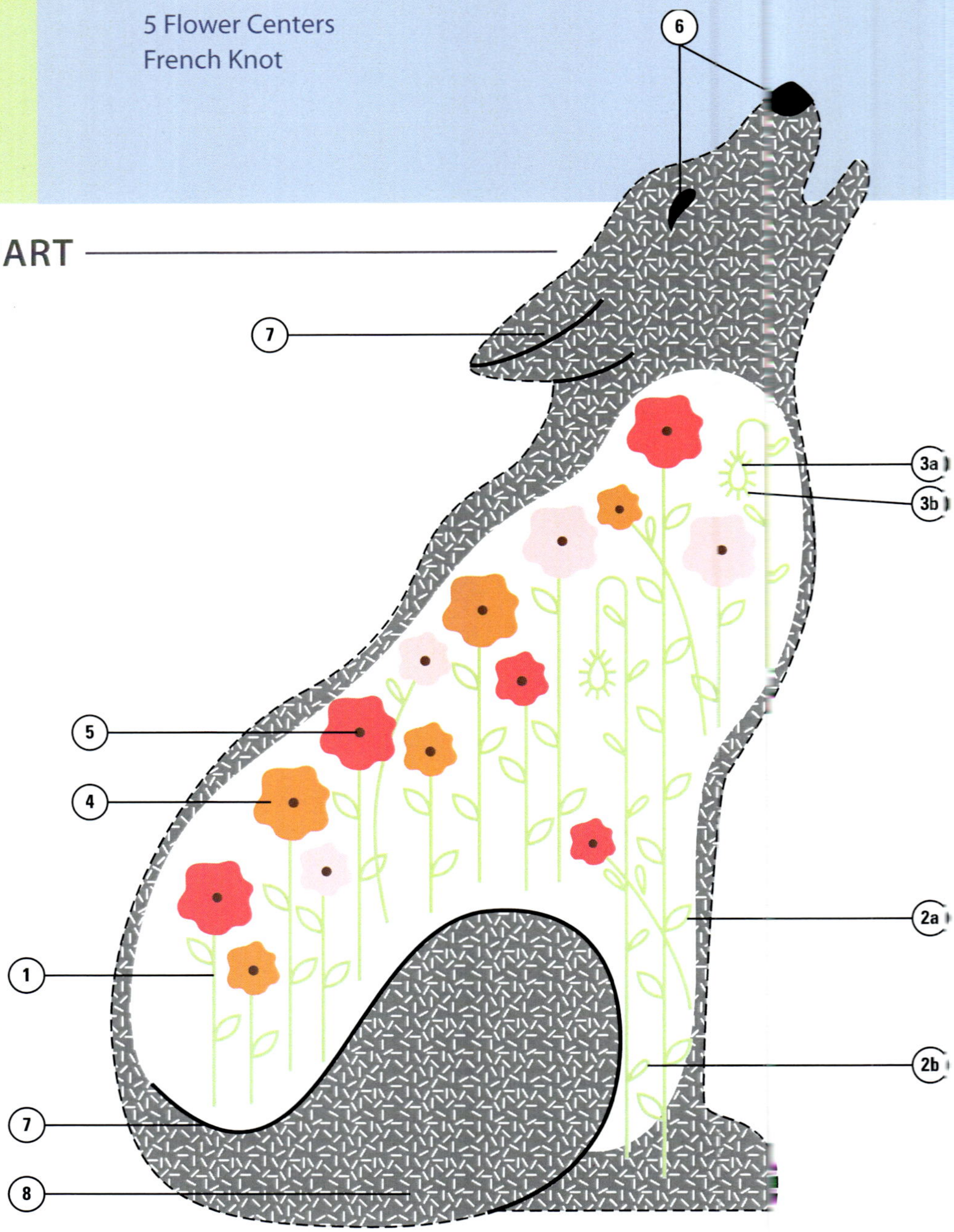

Embroidery Instructions

Do all of the embroidery stitching in the order listed on the Stitch Key.
All colors refer to DMC embroidery floss.
All embroidery uses three strands of embroidery floss.

WOLF PATTERN

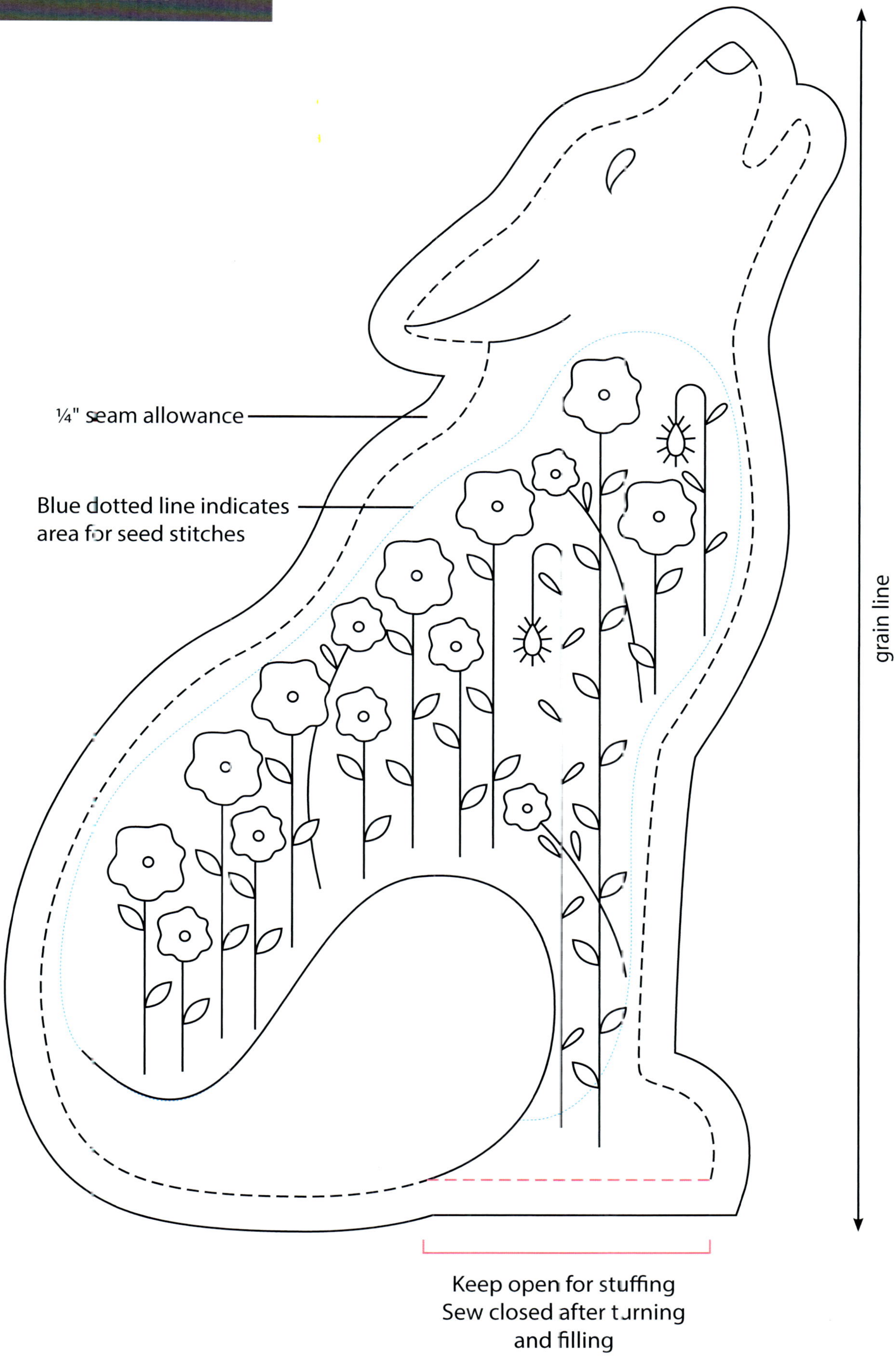

GENERAL INSTRUCTIONS

Fabrics

The critters in this book have been made with premium bleached muslin, both front and back. You could also choose to make them with premium cotton, linen, or any fabric that is similar in weight and strength to premium muslin.

You could also choose to use a printed or solid colored fabric for the backs of your critters. A calico or plaid print would give them a cute homespun look or you could tea or coffee stain bleached muslin for a vintage look.

Remember to launder all fabrics before use.

Supplies

- ☐ Embroidery hoop, 7" round
- ☐ Embroidery needle, size 3 to 5 or crewel needle, size 2
- ☐ Water-soluble or disappearing fabric marker
- ☐ Pencil
- ☐ Scissors
- ☐ Straight pins
- ☐ Sewing needle
- ☐ Sewing thread to match fabric
- ☐ Wooden turning and stuffing stick
- ☐ Needle nose tweezers
- ☐ Polyester fiberfill
- ☐ Magnifier (if desired)

Tips For Success

- Double stitch around sensitive areas like small ears and pointed noses to reinforce before turning and stuffing.
- Remember to clip all inward facing curves and corners before turning and stuffing.
- Black embroidery floss can bleed slightly when wet. If you plan to use a water-soluble marker I recommend soaking the whole skein of black floss in warm water and then allowing it to dry before use.
- None of the projects in this book use more than one skein of DMC embroidery floss. You should be able to make all 12 of the critters with just one skein of each of the colors except you'll need two skeins each of #14 light green and #3863 light brown which are both used more frequently.
- All embroidery is done using 3 strands of floss.
- French knots in this book are 2 needle wraps and a large French knot is 3 needle wraps.

Important Note: Do not cut out the shape of the animal until Step 5!

Seed stitched fur is indicated by shaded areas on the Embroidery Chart. This is meant to be random and you can stitch as much or as little fur as desired. Use the photograph of the critter as your guide. Start in a place such as the nose or muzzle and work your way outwards from there, following the lines of the body. Think about the direction the fur would grow in each area of the body or truly random seed stitches going every which way would make a cute fuzzy look.

Step-by-Step Instructions

The following step-by-step instructions apply to all 12 of the critter projects. Please refer to the project pages for each critter for individual details, materials and special instructions.

1. To transfer the pattern, use a water-soluble or disappearing marker to trace the dashed sewing line, the solid outer line, and the turquoise dotted line (indicates seed stitch area) onto the right side of the fabric using a light table or a sunny window. **Do not** trace the grain line or any text. Be sure the grain line arrow on the pattern is aligned with the lengthwise grain of the fabric. Use a pencil to *very lightly* trace the embroidery details onto the right side of the fabric.

2. Place the fabric securely into an embroidery hoop and do all of the embroidery in the order as listed on the Stitch Key. All embroidery in this book uses three strands of DMC embroidery floss in the colors noted on the Color Key.

3. After the embroidery is complete, pin the front and back fabrics together with right sides facing each other.

4. Sew by hand or machine along the sewing line, leaving the indicated opening for stuffing. Securely backstitch at both sides of the opening to strengthen the seams.

5. Trim the seam allowance to ¼" all around the critter. You may need to trim the seam allowance to 3⁄16" in tight areas such as the ears and tails for easier turning before stuffing.

6. Clip all of the inward facing corners and curves as close to the sewing line as possible.

7. Turn the critter right side out using a turning stick and needle nose tweezers where needed.

8. Run the critter under cold tap water until the marker disappears. Dry flat on a towel.

9. Stuff with polyester fiberfill starting with the smallest sections such as the ears and tail.

10. Tuck in the seam allowance at the opening and sew closed with needle and thread.

Enjoy your new critter and have fun making them all!

Stitch Diagrams

Come up at odd numbers and go down at even numbers.

French Knot

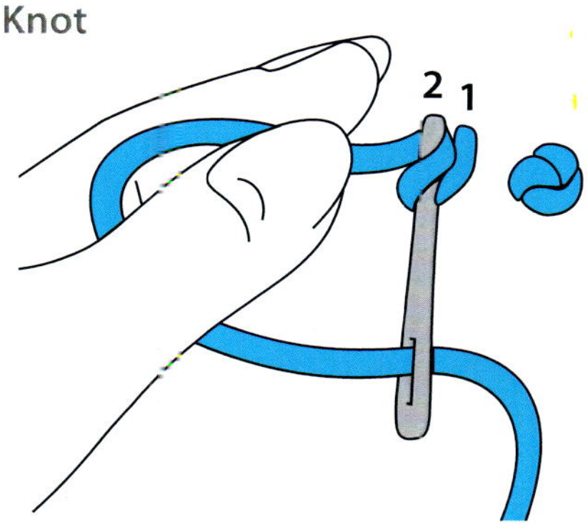

Lazy Daisy Stitch

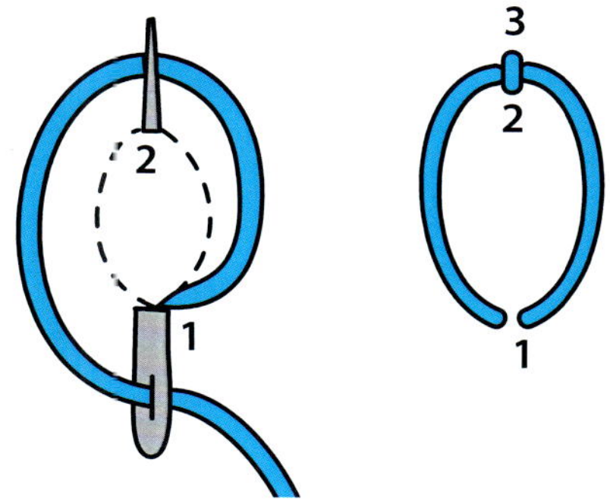

Long and Short Stitch A

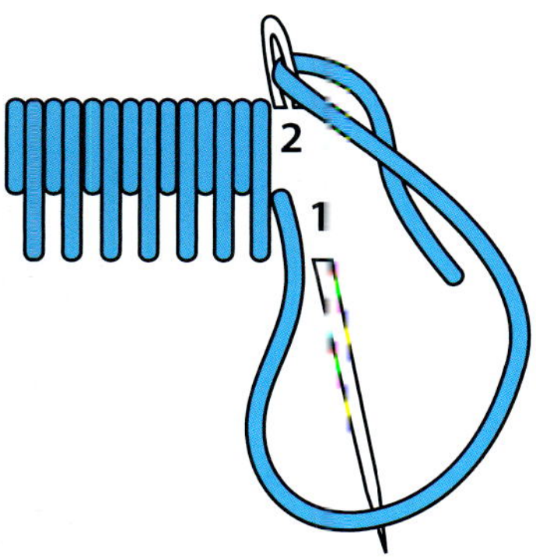

Long and Short Stitch B

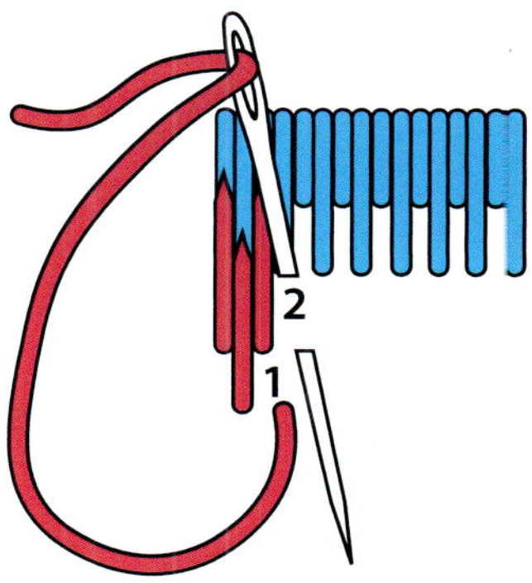

Long and Short Stitch C

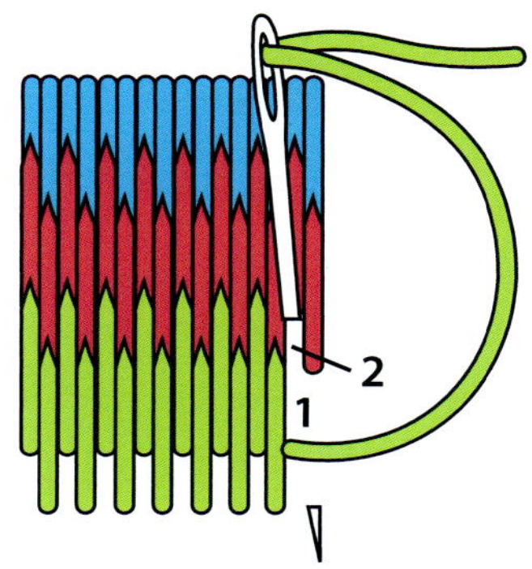

atin Stitch

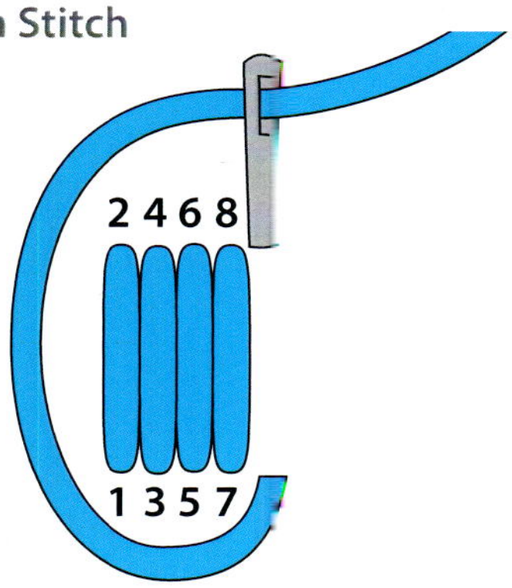

Seed Stitch

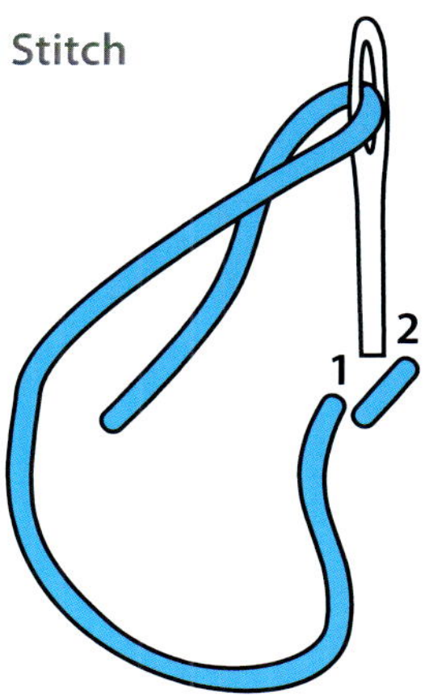

Stem Stitch

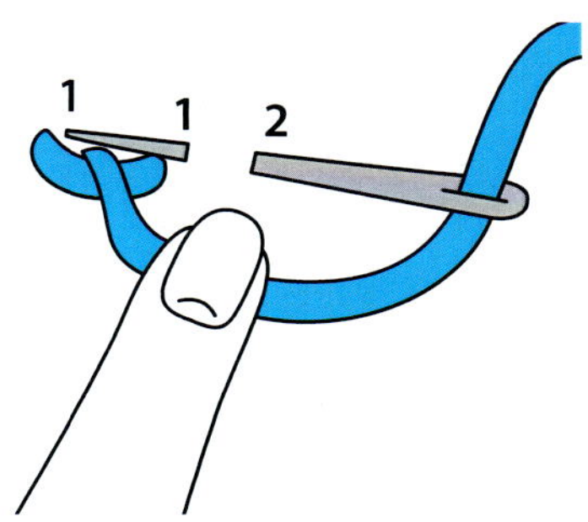

Straight Stitch

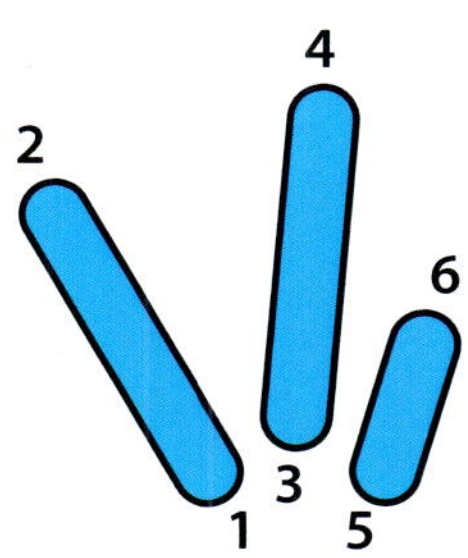

Show us what you're working on!

Share your project photos with us on social media.
Tag us @leisureartsinc or use #leisurearts

Production Team: Publishing Manager – Megan Copeland; Technical Editor – Lisa Lancaster; Graphic Artist – Michael Puckett; Photo Stylist Lori Wenger; Photographer – Jason Masters.

Made in U.S.A.